BOA
EDITIONS
LIMITED

ELEGY WITH A GLASS

OF WHISKEY

by Crystal Bacon

Winner, 2003 A. Poulin, Jr. Poetry Prize
Selected by Stephen Dunn

ELEGY WITH A GLASS OF WHISKEY

Poems by

CRYSTAL BACON

Foreword by Stephen Dunn

➤➤◄◄

A. Poulin, Jr. New Poets of America Series, No. 26

BOA EDITIONS, LTD. ➤➤◄◄ ROCHESTER, NY ➤➤◄◄ 2004

First Edition
04 05 06 07 7 6 5 4 3 2 1

Publications by BOA Editions, Ltd.—
a not-for-profit corporation under section 501 (c) (3)
of the United States Internal Revenue Code—
are made possible with the assistance of grants from
the Literature Program of the New York State Council on the Arts,
the Literature Program of the National Endowment for the Arts,
the Sonia Raiziss Giop Charitable Foundation,
the Lannan Foundation,
as well as from the Mary S. Mulligan Charitable Trust,
the County of Monroe, NY,
Ames-Amzalak Memorial Trust,
and The CIRE Foundation.

Cover Design: Dan Wangelin
Cover Art: "Whiskey" by Chris Pelletiere. Courtesy of the artist.
Interior Design and Typesetting: Richard Foerster
Manufacturing: United Graphics, Inc.
BOA Logo: Mirko

LIBRARY OF CONGRESS CATALOGING-IN-PUBLICATION DATA

Bacon, Crystal, 1955–
  Elegy with a glass of whiskey : poems / by Crystal Bacon ; foreword by Stephen Dunn.
    p. cm. — (A. Poulin, Jr. new poets of America series ; v. 26)
  ISBN 1-929918-53-4 (alk. paper)
    I. Title. II. Series.

PS3602.A353E43 2004
811'.6—dc22

                                                                2003023846

NATIONAL
ENDOWMENT
FOR THE ARTS

State of the Arts

NYSCA

BOA Editions, Ltd.
Thom Ward, Editor
H. Allen Spencer, Chair
A. Poulin, Jr., President & Founder (1976–1996)
260 East Avenue, Rochester, NY 14604
www.boaeditions.org

*for Larry Levis
and Judith Page*

Contents

↠ III ↞

↠↞

Foreword

The way a poem sounds can be more ornamental than a string of images that merely depict. We distrust what we hear because it feels too harmonious or too divorced from what's being said. A poem's sonics, at their best, are more than just proof that the poet has a good ear; they validate that she inhabits and embodies her material, suggesting what Jacques Maritain calls the offering of an "inner melody"—a music, if you will, of the soul. This is what the true lyric poet gives us.

Crystal Bacon, in fact, has a good ear. But it's clear her poems are simultaneously driven by a need to find language for feelings not easily named *and* the search for cooperative sounds. The combination makes for a compelling lyric authority.

Her book's epigraph, from D. H. Lawrence, sets the stage: ". . . and Persephone herself is but a voice / or a darkness invisible enfolded in the deeper dark . . ." It points to two of Bacon's central concerns: a consciousness of Thanatos as a galvanizing force, if not a guide, to living well; and the suggestion that crucial speech emerges from our dark, layered places. It is from such places that Bacon tries to invent and to speak.

"No Flowers" begins with an invocation: "Rise up, pale shoot, white flame / from under fertile leaves of March." And it ends with an assertion, as mysterious as it is clear:

> The bodies of boys, imagined,
> waver vaporous over the ground;
> stained shoots curled in darkness,
> pale blades thrust up from snow.

We cannot be exactly sure what these "stained shoots" yield, except a kind of difficult birth. But in other poems Bacon allows herself a clearer sense of affirmation out of darkness. Here are two excerpts from "Outlook":

I've begun to love the cold, the slick bitter seed
of this life: brittle, brilliant. . . .

I've said goodbye to death, to love; a father, a few fine
bodies large and small. I've leaned my tired elbows here
on the narrow ledge, and held my head and drunk my cups.
And it's this nakedness I've come to love, sheer as breath.

And this from "Elegy with a Glass of Whisky in Its Hand," the fine poem
that commences the book.

                    . . . You were a hinge on a frozen door

open now, easy now. There is a light on inside the house.
I'll go in and live in the yellow warmth. I'll pour a drink;
the words will wait, are waiting, to be born.

Aided throughout by various Greek myths, the elegiac and the sensual
commingle in ways that become characteristic of *Elegy with a Glass of
Whiskey,* indeed of Crystal Bacon's poetic enterprise. Whether she adopts
a persona or mediates in her own voice, it's clear by book's end that such
tactics provide Bacon the latitudes of being her various self/selves, an
androgyne separated and seeking. We are the beneficiaries of such
beautifully heard musings.

—Stephen Dunn

ELEGY WITH A GLASS OF WHISKEY

+>-<+

. . . and Persephone herself is but a voice
or a darkness invisible enfolded in the deeper dark . . .
—D. H. Lawrence, "Bavarian Gentians"

Elegy with a Glass of Whiskey in Its Hand

Orion is standing on his one good leg;
it's a long journey and endless to where we are:
the winter sky over New Jersey, North America.

The dogs rustle in the weeds sniffing out what has gone
and left its indelible mark in the darkness: rabbit, cat,
small things scurrying into the earth for cover.

I can wait; the sky rises around me, above the roofs,
the trees, and for a moment, I might be anywhere
but here: a town with two traffic lights, one grain elevator,

the rich nausea of cattle dozing on their feet.
I might be living in myself, part of the breath that steams
in the night. I might be home in that other place

pocked by rock and trees where I can breathe
knowing who I am and why. But tonight,
there is work in my mind, work before

and behind me stretching out farther than I can see.
So I whisper a whistle into the dark, and the dogs
shape themselves out of the night.

★

I saw you once, standing on one leg, at the back of a room,
the wallflower at ego's ball. But you
still lean there in your white shirt, black jacket;
formal, then, clean. Your red hands in your jeans,
your black mustache. I could have painted you there
by the coffee urn except that we spoke and you were real.

*

Mementos gather dust. Or I pack and unpack them
in the endless journey between northern point
and northern point. Always the last sign of settlement:

photographs in cheap frames, a cup, some stones
the bald bear that belonged to my sister,
sensible enough to let things go.

I am writing to you, man in the picture, man with the glass
raised for my camera. The glass is a plastic cup
foaming with fresh champagne. You mug for me.

*

When you died, your death was like ice in a glass
of scotch. It melted clear against the tawny
color of the light. It spread and spread like rain

traveling for days across the continent. It left its footprint,
Orion's peg leg pocking the face of different places:
California, Virginia, North Carolina, Nova Scotia

and everywhere anyone had known you. I did not
know you. You were a night sky, you were winter
in its shabby coat. You were a hinge on a frozen door

open now, easy now. There is a light on inside the house.
I'll go in and live in the yellow warmth. I'll pour a drink;
the words will wait, are waiting, to be born.

→-◄-

I

Persephone Redux

I want to tell you everything.
I was born in a hazy farm town,
attended by the resident drunk.
He snipped the skin that bound tongue to mouth,
considered circumcision.

I was Episcopal, a Girl Scout.
Something in the hot green cotton of that dress
one day led me to the nave
through the open door's half-heart:
bells' bleeding sound.

→>-<←

Kore: For Girls

after Calasso

In the eye of the eye is the pupil, the kore,
and the pupil is the girl, the body of the earth
caught looking at Narcissus, caught looking at himself,
swept away into the flower, swept into the earth,
to the place of no body.

In the body of the kore is the snake and the bull,
the girl with two heads, with horns, with scented cheeks,
the marriage of perfection, the snake of the water,
the slither toward darkness, god of the belly,
of the sea, the unseen.

The bull of the earth, one hoof in the water
to steal away the girl on its back over the waves,
one foot in the water, hand in the hair of the bull.
The girl, the pupil, who looks into the flower,
the earth splitting beneath her, into the face of the unseen,
seeing and being seen.

She leaves the surface, peers from the beard of darkness,
eats the shadowy fruit; the girl gone from the earth
leaves a hole, gives blood to death, leaves the cloak
of her absence, snake and bull out of balance, thrust open,
the whole of this life and its death, the looking and the seen.

→►◄←

Like an Animal

I want to fuck you like an animal;
I want to feel you from the inside.
      —Nine Inch Nails

So often did he come that way, on the hoof,
there's a word, Tauroparthenos: a virgin
dedicated to the bull. Always first came the dream,
the veil of epiphany: the bellowing bull, crazed cow,
the god and the girl. Is it any wonder we dream that way?
See in the lover's buttocks the haunches of the deer?

This is the origin of tragedy:
Dionysus gave the gift of wine to Icarius
who dreamed he killed the goat who ate the vine.
No wonder, then, the shepherds who drank with Icarius,
the dopey, suspicious shepherds, thought him a thief.
The goatskin drained, they stomped him to death,
slowly enough for him to remember the dream,
himself, run through with a cooking spit.

Sallust says, These things never happened,
but are always. You know the tree's rise,
the thunder of the blood, how the goat lows
just before the knife. Bend over, something says,
bow down to the wind, belly to the earth,
the god is the future, coming up behind you.

→►◄←

Dreaming of Anne Frank

1

Her face hovers in the windshield of my Volkswagen,
arms folded across her breasts, her desk;
her eyebrows knitted in her school girl way,
she refuses to wear a seat belt.

I run stop signs. It is night,
April or May, the liberation of Auschwitz impending,
over a lifetime away. I hunch forward,
my arms on the wheel where the air bag sleeps
like the future. I feel unheld, cut loose,
the hum of German engineering tidy beneath me,
efficiency, like train wheels, gripping the road.

2

My nephew asks for a story for a class assignment
about a myth passed down in our family.
In my sister's kitchen, I have forgotten Anne Frank.

There is a girl, I begin, a beautiful girl,
with a hunchback. People would stare
and point and the girl would cry.
Why are they staring? she asks her mother.
Because you are a beautiful angel,
they are staring at your beauty.
(Anne Frank is dozing.)
One day, the mother dies.
Uh oh, (my sister turns from the sink).
Yes, I say. The father marries an Evil Woman
who hates the hunchbacked daughter.

Still, people stare and point. Why are they staring,
the girl asks no one in particular.
They're staring at your ugly hump, the Evil One says.
That night the girl cries herself to sleep.
The next morning, when her timid father goes into her room
to awaken her, he finds her dead. As he lifts her
from her bed, her hunch opens and wings spread
from her back as she lifts off into heaven.

His face is like a windowshade someone has snapped.
Mom, he says, why didn't *you* remember that story?

3

(Anne Frank is smashing batteries. It's dirty work, there are boxes to sort:
the copper, the magnets, whatever stuff is in there. It's dirty, she coughs.
Her hands are busy, her hands are angels fluttering over the field troops,
over the batteries in their kits. She can work and talk at the same time.
She has friends, she is smiling, she is sixteen and believes in everything.)

4

This is not a dream. I remember the stories:

A girl with white hair, angelic,
a purple birthmark over half her face,
her mother, a Jew, killed them both
before the dogs at the gate.

5

Anne Frank, I love my red shiny car.
I put the top down and drive with the American wind in my hair.
I am trying to remember stories to tell this boy.
My sister and I grew up with the story of Kaspar Hauser,
locked in a basement. His hair and nails grew
like the hair and nails of the dead—

there was a felt doll of him in my cousins' bedroom
in an eave where we used to hide. Anne Frank. Kaspar Hauser.
What was the story? Felt made from the hair of Jews, I will not tell him
 this.

6

Trains and fence and soot. When I think of Anne Frank I think of her
 teeth.
Her small, slightly twisted teeth, under thin wet lips.
Of her hair, dark and fine as ash, on her brow.
A school picture. One small face, as in a dream.

We learned to say:
Der wind, der wind, das Himlische kind.
(The wind, the wind, the heavenly child.)
Morgen, morgen, nur nicht heute,
(Tomorrow, tomorrow never today,)
sagen alle faule Leute,
(only the lazy people say.)
The engine fires, and hums; Anne Frank,
all the industrious people of the fatherland.

->-<-

Still Life with Christ

Payday I bring home the big scary Jesus that hung
in the gallery for a month. He's propped up,
frowning passenger, beside me. We stop
to buy some bourbon. All above in the white sky
rain withholds itself like a repentant lover.

I hang the painting, *Christ-head,*
where something smaller was. He doesn't mind
the new perspective. He's like a fish,
fresh from the dime-store tank.
It's a wall of miracles! Big scary Jesus
paired with a dog-headed crucifix
that bears a quote from Lorca:
vine a este mundo con ojos
(I came into this world with eyes)
y me voy sin ellos
(and I go without them).

I rake leaves pooled by the curb,
cartoon-hands
in rust and tan and red gone wrong.
It's short work.
The trees hold stubbornly to what must pass.
Limbs catch and whine in the night,
they'll fall, rotten through and through.

The yard clear for now, the painted lips of impatiens
seem about to speak. I sit back and roll a cigarette,
drink the bourbon. I want to touch the sound of wind
in the trees. I came into this world with eyes.
The cigarette burns close to my skin. I roll it into a ball
of nothing, flick it to the leaves. I go in,
lay my hands on the palette-knifed heart of Jesus.

→>-<←

Getting Fixed

The metaphysician said my chakra needed feeding,
and Venus was about to go out of retrograde.
I needed to attend to my relationship corner,
court Aphrodite back into my home.

In addition to something green growing tall,
he recommended rose quartz in the soil,
and the water poured right over it.
Later, in the evening, the yellow bath.

So I ran the tub hot,
filling the near-empty honey jar
to rinse the sticky remnants from its sides.
Then turmeric, ground mustard, a squeeze of lemon
from a pimpled, plastic fruit. And there I soaked, stewed.
Yellow water easing inside to stoke me up.

The Virgin kept suggesting herself
but that was just the music of Hildegard from Bingen,
popular now with the dreamy set.
And the 99-cent-store night lamp of Mary
plugged into my vanity mirror.

I hunkered on my futon couch, and waited.
I imagined inside myself a tiny, stubborn baby.
Outside the wind fingered the temple bell,
and the last gold leaves from the maples.

→>-<-

Waking Late

Saturday (the clock downstairs has caught
itself up, the chimes gone awry, come back again).
Waking as from a dream: a matte-wet night,
the beloved face come close, the town quaint,
rain falling, like a backdrop in a film:
a sheen black as plastic,
wet but not wet, something else.

In the kitchen, water runs cold
into the metal pot; beyond the window
a neighbor's fence, the sun a rind around
the blue balloon of water tower. The cold
creeps in, and all the sleeping towns
of the mind send out their messengers of doom:
a thousand tiny Greeks from a single horse.

→>-<←

Coupling

This, of course, is how they came to be,
the sex and the death, the heart's quick promise:
I do, I do, I do, dying slow as a bird in snow
as seed and egg meet and accept.

Two boys in the world two years apart.
The first fine-boned as china, the flush
of his blood deep as reddest tea.
The other growing into his flesh
behind its own curtain. A slow change
from infancy's meager scope
into the magician's flowing cape:
the feet of a man carrying the heart
of the boy. How they grow:
into the confusion of bodies
stretching and flowing around themselves.
Boys in their beds, all their small deaths
coiled inside the heat of sleep.

→>-<+

No Flowers

1

Rise up, pale shoot, white flame
from under fertile leaves of March.
Cast off those fetid clothes, your skin
that filament you strained against.

2

A boy's body dissolved at the foot of a tree.
His neck, or what the neck had been:
muscle, bone, skin still free from stubble.

Into the woods, the drowsy boy,
the length of rope. No one noticed
the missing pills, the metal box,
a boy's effects: cassette, a sketch,
the wallet and watch. No one saw him go.

That's how he came to be
April shoots, strange garden
transfigured in a grove of trees.

3

The bodies of boys, imagined,
waver vaporous over the ground;
stained shoots curled in darkness,
pale blades thrust up from snow.

→>⊰←

Homeward

for Larry Levis 1946–1996

There's a song in my head tonight
from an old German torch
with the dubious moniker of Lolita.
My ship's called homeward, she sings,
mein schiff heisst heimweg. I'm reading your poems
about holiness, about space filled by what's
ineffable. And I wonder whether you felt the kick
in your heart coming, just the way the horse in your poem
both feels and doesn't feel the angel in his ear, in his brain.
If, like Van Gogh, your poison was in you
from years and years of absence.
Is that what you died wondering?
But what if your soul is that angel,
not the cast-off dress, but the warmth
which filled it. Can you blame me
for wanting your voice in my ear:
listen, here's a story about the mist
in the corner of a field . . .

+>-<+

Sunday: Of Proportions

While our guest is in the shower, my love and I slide
into the still warm bed; icy feet, hands skimming
goose flesh, the flannel sheets muffle our foreplay, laughter.

       Her hair is like a Greek statue,
or David sculpted in marble dust,
       her musky smell mixed with last night's
perfume: Dune, which she calls Desire.
       Her head in my hands, she slips her breasts
along mine and wonders aloud about yardwork.
       Look at my nose, I say. The canary peeps,
fluffed up against the cold.

This is marriage: sex on the run between chores.
The night's reserved for sleep. I hold her head
and she worries about the birds. She'll go down
into the basement, turn boards into feeders
for suet and seed. I'm dreaming up-country décor:
birdhouses made of worn-out wood, new from old.

After she gets up, I lie wrapped naked in the bed
staring out the window through myopic eyes,
the trees impressionistic, balletic. She's off to shower,
to keep the world in order.

Outside, her rock garden settles
into the chilling ground. The dahlia has turned black.
If we look back too long, we'll turn, not to salt or stone,
but bitter. She arranges stones in the yard for the light
to play . . . Stones? They're boulders, rocks, meteors
the sea throws back. Licks and kisses until they open
mouths of their own. Not stones like those I pocket
wet and precious: mica-flecked heart, or orange
pocked with green. They dry into a mystery.

She lugs them up the slipping hill from the bay.
Here everything metes itself out to the sea:
rain into run-off, soil, tree, boulder.
She brings back history, body-sized compaction,
arranges it in the yard in simulated action.

If she looks back she'll wither. The dahlia gives me epic delusions:
sits hunched like Orpheus himself or the sorry Eurydice
blackened, sodden on her perch. My love will mow it down.

→>-<←

To Thanatos, with Love

Why shouldn't I say it? I'm thrilled to be alive,
flying along on the outer drive
in the open car, my love by my side.

I think about the ones who've died
left alone in their spotty shame—
love's the candle that eats the flame,
a pillow, the lover who cradles the head—
too many now to keep intact
their names.
           The drive, in fact,
to live is the same as the drive to die:
to glide over the honed edge
a spy against the dead
like an eye wrapped by hair,
wind-whipped against the glare.

→-◄◄

II

Elegy with a Fiction in It

Stavros, storyteller, where are you now? The silence sings your name,
its own melancholic chorus: Stavros, Stavros, Stavros.

There is snow on the ground. The Aegean is a memory
lost in a dream. Tell me the story of that café,

before the war. The boys slouched in chairs,
their dusty shoes beneath bare ankles: bones small

as a child's marble, pick-up sticks. But it was not a game.
Outside, the machine of change clucked up the static

that stuck in its archaic throat. Words wavered
like the air under summer's bald eye.

Who was I in that story? A girl watching sheets dry
across the square. A woman bathing a baby's olive skin

in a balm of oil and water by an open window.
The crone in black rags telling the rosary in a shadow.

Stavros, tell me a story. Did the boy with the broken tooth,
with the motorbike, turn away that day, leave the table

stuck with cups, humming with flies? Did he shuffle out
and take a cloud of street with him, the girl forgotten?

He's in the snap of laundry on a summer's day,
in the eyes of that stranger lighting a cigarette.

Today silence sang your name to me, and I thought
to ask you, Stavros, if you have seen him since he died.

→-←

Casual Man

It hung up front in the Dresden Row Frenchy's,
something seventies in olive polyester,
hip-length jacket double-breasted,
satin lapels. It brought out the man in me.

My friends say I'm a gay man trapped
in a lesbian's body. And that's true enough:
I wear a dress as well as the best of them.

Even so, I'm most at home with those brethren
of the well-groomed. It's not pretty: I'm not,
but I dress well and there's an arch to me,
my pelvis, perhaps, a pivot point.

It's not drag, not cliché: I can wear a man's suit
on my woman's frame. On the edge of the flesh,
the body's sudden vapor.

→>—<←

Blame It on My Youth

1

Do you prefer the dream or the reality?
the teacher asked a dozen years ago.
What I remember most was the passion
of my defense, how much better,
how much more real, the dream was sure to feel.

2

I'm driving my convertible
on a four-lane road at night
toward the Jersey shore. It's early March,
the kind of weather that promises more.
At seventy-five miles an hour, the air
makes my head ache, like the *Ice
Cold Beer* in neon,
the only light for miles.
                              I'm listening
to Chet Baker, wizened wunderkind,
a whistley tape of slow-drag love songs,
Cole Porter on heroin. Chet's voice
is the same eerie key as his horn,
thirty years together, like married people,
they sound alike. Those bad dentures
make his sibilants slide so he seems to say,
If I cried a little bit when first I heard the truce,
don't blame it on my heart,
blame it on my use.
                              And in the mindless,
obsessive way I live in this music, I whisper
along with him, draw the same breaths,
shape his guileless impediments.

3

This may be the dream. Alone, at forty,
in an open car through the night, despite
the safety of destination. The fog hits
after half an hour, mists the windshield,
settles on my hair, pale flame
in the corner of the mirror. For miles,
dim lights, yellow as cats' eyes,
turn off to other ways.

I slow at the red haloes
of traffic lights, downshift, until I coast
to a roll before the crossroads, the green,
and resume my speed. After "Almost Blue,"
the tape plays its soundless message,
one I don't want to decode.

4

I remember Chet barefoot,
horn dangling in one hand,
walking a balustrade in Santa Monica,
then playing *Zingaro*, slow and haunting
as a heart in the night, when each beat lobs
its load of blood, thick as a hand in a glove.

I know in his voice is the boy who's lived inside me,
the boy I am sometimes, all blood and muscle,
silent as smoke, heat going cold.

5

It was a kiss the teacher used to illustrate the problem,
of which would we prefer. I have been kissed
a thousand-thousand times since then.
It's all the same in the end. The sky goes dark,
then goes dark again.

→-◄-

Between the Beating Clocks

Cheap, made to travel,
they throw their tiny drumbeats
out in stereo from the bed table
to the work station. They fill the room
with a music of ticking, only just out
of synch. It could be maddening,
Poe's buried heart, or that spinning toy,
a shuttlecock, racheting over nylon cord
slap slap slap. Or the body's racket
in the blood, the slow tock of sex undone.
It soothes, they do, soothe, in the ping-pong
rhythm of their second-clapping hands:
red line, a vein between this and that.

→−◁−

Waiting for Fever to Pass

I'll start with the cup: outside the color of cotton candy,
inside the aqua of travel-poster Aegean.
A catalogue of patience, waiting: the coffee boils,
sputters on the cook-top, adds itself to a burnt brown ring.

*

Pick any street, Dumaine, Lafayette, Camino Real.
Cobblestone gives way to tile, Spanish double shutter doors
to French balcony and iron wrought into corn.

Over here, mulatto society danced, octoroons mingling with quads.
The French envisioned a city on a lake, never imagining mosquitoes, or
the Typhus. Louis Quatorze gave New Orleans away at cards.

I prefer the summers here: one hundred degrees,
one hundred percent humidity, grass grows up out of the street,
sweat holds me like a cup of steam.

Once walking along Esplanade near the Market, I found a cup
on the curb. Pink and blue like the small tabletop in the basement
of my childhood. Sky-blue pink, my father called it.
How guilty I felt taking the handle already hot to my touch,
the coffee, days old, dried in the bottom. But I knew it.
Knew the flaw along the rim would fit its kiss to my lips.

*

Growing up there were figs. How strange, I know it now,
to grow figs, eat figs, know figs in New Jersey. My father
would cut back the bush, tie it under tar paper in fall,
his "mother-in-law" he called it, though it was his mother who grew
the cutting in a coffee can until it was ready to transplant.

Summers, they were like golden buttocks, round and ripe,
. . . iridescent! And bees bore lazily into them—
globes of sugar, wombs of seedy dripping flesh.

★

That summer living on Burgundy Street (Bur-GUN-dy, they say)
there was a small backyard fenced all around with a hedge of figs.
Bushes so tall it took a ladder to get where the ripest ones hung,
up where the sun spread out like a stain.

Only Yankees sunbathe in New Orleans. In minutes I was slick as cut
        fruit,
sweat and oil and the plastic straps of the chair—my eyes filled
with endless flashes of light against black lids.

The figs—a box of green heat—their tough hand-shaped leaves
dusty, resistant. Ducking inside something like shade, not cool,
no, "stippled," deflected light. The figs disappointing—small
and hard mostly—even up high where the scrotum-blue bottoms
gave way to golding green—small. Something less weighty
less fecund in the hang from stem. But did I pick them? Do I know
that they were sweet, how crowded in Tupperware
they crushed and wept tears solid as honey.

But what about the cup? The coffee baked in—
maybe only one day's heat? Yes, I was walking, it was
afternoon and I was walking in and out of palm-shaded darkness
on Esplanade. Two o'clock, the sun invisibly bright,
I was getting away, "running." Walking down these streets
that run off the Avenue. I passed thick Spanish doors
and heard Patsy Cline crooning *Crazy*, and I knew at that moment,
it was just for me. I stopped and leaned against the door and it yielded.
Inside was cool and dim as a stage set. There was a fat woman behind
        the bar
in rollers and a muumuu, two toothless men, a black boy
thin as a whisper wiping down the mirror.

My hair seemed to smolder, my skin rang like a bell
after Matins. I straddled a stool and drank a beer.

Outside, I went back to Esplanade and found the cup
and looking behind me took it up with the guilt in it
and went home.

→-◄

Mythopoeia

Sleep lifts like mist from windows.
It's clear: no need to solve the mystery
which knit my face into a fist,
open now, awake. It's cold beyond the bed.
I dress for winter: leggings and a sweater.
Outside the window you pass
carrying a spade of soil from one bed to another.

The snapdragons are finally asunder,
their purple and yellow had survived
even last week's freeze. Now
it's time for bulbs. As you cross the yard
your face wears the look of imagining Spring,
of vision, or faith. As if what
goes under the ground, hard hearts
of hyacinth, crocus, daffodil,
will surely blossom, surely mean
something inexpressible today.

In the spare room, paperwhites
tangle their whiskery roots
amid beach glass, stones:
the boy, Narcissus, dangling
his hair in the mirrored pool.
By Christmas their exotic smell
of desire, fleeting beauty,
will mingle with the chill air.
The earth, in winter's frozen beard,
keeps breathing. Nothing has to die
for this, something has to die.
In the turn of the year
this promise keeps us alive.

➤━◄

Leap Year

February, and the groundhog
shied earlier:
a blizzard hit
after milder weather.

But now it's Leap Day
—or Sadie Hawkins Day
when Dogpatch erupts
with pillow-busted

Daisy Maes hotly
pursuing Abners.
At any rate, it's spring;
or nearly. March's wind

swims in grit and leaves
the house smelling fresh
even with windows closed.
It's spring, the ground's thawed,

snow's gone. Along the house
side, south side, daffodils
push their infant penis
heads up from inhospitable

soil; paradox of nature:
brown lackluster and green,
a shade couture defies . . .
And there it lies, dead,

backs up the heart,
makes the skin attempt to crawl—
squirrel I'd say.
More than dead, decayed

in part, displayed on leaf bed
like art: the head slender,
eyes blue and belly upturned
pinkly, tender.

It takes me back.
Something there is in nature
that doesn't love at all,
I think, bastardizing the lesson.

But it's the season: soon
resurrection. If there's providence
in the fall of a sparrow, why not squirrel?
Later, the TV tells of Mark,

dead abroad; Muslims
refuse him into Italy.
He's packed in pork, comes safely home.
What won't you touch?

I slid the squirrel into newspaper's
center; I'm here to tell its heft.
There's a place now, clean,
beneath the leaves, bereft of death.

-+->-<+-

Hinged

In the sea-dark bed my hands find your flesh
fluid, oceanic—manatee?—and
the scar from sternum to pelvis, the place
where you are joined to you: where the selkie
might hide the other skin that's tucked inside.
Or if you are the root of me, the seed's
pod meets itself there. But you're no hydra,
no mermaid, your liquid spine hooked side to
side to ribs rearranged since that impact
of steel on steel that spun you out, that dropped
you here where you have healed. And now we wake
in this simplicity of touch to find
our love is hinged to your survival.

→-◄-

Mysteries

Out of the woods, the ground's all rock, the same
ash gray broken by landmark boulders: the
dropped shoulder jetty to the north, smaller
now in the tide, a split fist to the south,
the way I walk tonight.

I come for wood washed up from somewhere else:
one-by-twos, mostly, one-by-fours. Faces
washed smooth, paint rubbed deep into grain. Odd bits
of boats and their tackle. I have a box
piling up in my basement for winter
projects—birdhouses made of found objects.

But as I walk the shore's hard way, big rock
to big rock, minding my ankles, eyes fast
on the edge of the buggy dusk, I half
expect a mystery in the tangle
where sea meets trees. More than the familiar
wreckage of coastal economy. Some
dead or mangled thing. But I am spared.

My arms full, mosquitoes thick around me,
I turn back, reverse the walk from rock to
rock to where the marker points my way home
where the telephone rings. Someone's daughter
dropped in a car two hundred feet. Her window

met a boulder. She's alive,
her face a spider web of hairline seams
in time, with luck. Still, I'm shocked how death
defies the looked-for odds, itself a god.

→►◄←

Augury

I awoke February sixth, twelve years since my father died,
and my horoscope said, *There's little middle ground;*
your relationship either ends or begins today;
Aries figures.
                    In my dream,
the red-tailed hawk landed in my sleep,
the night spent above the bed's darker slumber,
moon-lit by snow. When you were born,
a red-tailed hawk circled three times
around your grandfather's head, the man called *man*
who is bigger than himself. You, the first sign,
ram born under the wings of the hawk.

My father slept into his final day:
exactly as they said his death wouldn't come.
My sister carried her first son
another seven months after my father died,
and he came in his ancient skin,
eyes made of blood and sex.

In morning, two worlds: slick rain of grackles
black on the blood-russet fence;
cardinals cluster at the feeder,
feathers fall with hulls into the snow.

→>—<-

Gift

Last night I wore the heart which left you,
great tuna of a man, like a fish on a board.
And there I leave you with your horny feet
cold evermore, naked, protruding from the sheet.

It was as a chanterelle, spongy orange fungus
common here under the North Atlantic's drear
softwood stands. Or an ear or lump of clay:
unformed it lay on my chest with two consorts.
I was ill, lost in the gloss of fever.

In the murky blankets my chest fell and rose,
fell and lay, then rose again under the febrile
spell of your tissue—your issue? Something of you
colored the scene like astigmatic points of light,
something you and not you as if the room could smile.

When it fibrillated and I gasped, that heart of yours,
fistlike patty-cake, a Zen clap to which my own flesh
answered, the air grew thick as teeth through which
I sought and found a gap, breathed, and slept.

→►◄←

Seamless

1

Inside an open car, the *Ave Maria*, poignant and pure;
smoke from a hand-rolled cigarette. A town wakes under deep fog,
falls away into misted harbors, cedar knees bent in oblation;
by afternoon, two lung-shaped clouds, mist
between them like ribs, like smoke inside.

2

I'm sitting on a balcony with my feet up on the rail,
green resin chair rocked back on two bowed legs.
My dungaree shorts, their seam beneath my tailbone,
a thorn that keeps me shifting. Design
makes things come together against strain.
My father sat all day, thirty feet in the air
bolting up the big beams of buildings. That knot
must have rubbed him raw.

3

This is the summer of my fortieth year.
I load the car and drive north and east and north
again, until I'm in another country, all rocks and shore.
In the woods are firs and hackmatack, alder and spruce.
It's still the *Ave Maria* I hear. The same song building itself
out of silence, calling and falling, sacred and sad.

I have a pouch of tobacco, a metal lighter. I love
the click of the lighter's lid, the heft in my hand,
its smooth case, the catch of the striking-wheel.

I roll the skinny cigarettes from scratch, strike the flint
and release the pale, oily flame until the sweet leaf burns.

Mornings, my lungs feel heavy, watery. I think too much
about cause and effect, ruin the joy of what I crave,
the drama of the red-embered eye, halo of gray-blue smoke around my
      head.

4

My father has been dead a dozen years. I'm not as young as I feel.
I've fabricated his youth from a photo: after the war,
outside the Music Bar with his buddies, neckties flapping
over their shoulders, Luckys in their pockets,
beer glasses in their hands. They're younger than I am now.

When my father drowned at last in his own lungs,
I phoned one of those men he hadn't seen in thirty years.
I said my name and that my father had died, he let out a cry,
apologized and the line went dead. Grief sits differently
wherever it lands. That old bachelor must've loved my father
in time that had not advanced for him: still twenty-three inside,
a guy with friends and tattoos and beer to drink, a boy
who never married, nobody's dad.

5

I roll another cigarette and palm the lighter,
The tiny cowgirl pinup on the front kicks up one red-booted leg
to show enameled thighs. Head cocked back,
her smile's wide as a pin-prick in the heart:
just big enough to let out what's been so long inside.

    →-◄-

Outlook

I've begun to love the cold, the slick bitter seed
of this life: brittle, brilliant. Even the bare trees
have embraced the ice: arms and fingers shelled
in diamond, in glass, and still they wave and click,
bend and freeze in the chill kiss of the wind.

I've cursed this view, backs of neighbors' houses;
the sheds, the tiered trunks of cars
low over graying tires, the screen door askew.

But the due-west exposure hangs the sun, this time of day,
below the yellow peak with brown eaves, the white boxed
tower. The trees, the blessing of trees I've also cursed:

acorns, a plague of leaves, threat of branches piercing
roof, laying low twelve feet of fence. They stand, needle true,
pointing always into the blue or white or thatch of sky;

they rise above the junk, the barking dogs, the baby's cry.
I've said good-bye to death, to love; a father, a few fine
bodies large and small. I've leaned my tired elbows here
on the narrow ledge, and held my head and drunk my cups.
And it's this nakedness I've come to love, sheer as breath.

→>◄-

1967: White Point Beach, Nova Scotia

and we're dressed all wrong.
My nine-year-old sister in her Easter coat
packed for the northern summer's chill.
And there am I in blue-flowered skirt,
navy-crested blazer, my wrists exposed,
yearning for something I hadn't yet known.
We're like sheep, grouped this way. Mother ewe
in her yellow traveling knits sturdy and full-front,
her head somehow too small, full thighs.
She's my age, the age I am now, my head too full,
my thighs uncracked by birth. Each of us perched off
to a farther side, faces unreadable, just before the snap.

★

This was not the vacation we'd planned. In a cheap hotel,
my father bent over to brush his teeth; his behind pushed out the door.
So, we took the Blue Nose Ferry to Yarmouth
where a steep, rock-walled sidewalk rolled to the bay.
It was the summer of love; I hummed "Ferry Cross the Mersey,"
dreaming a twelve-year-old's romance in that ocean-bound town.

★

Our Cabin is written in white photo album ink.
A Polaroid snapshot of a brown cedar bungalow.
Slate walkway, clover in the grass. Red enamel
on an Adirondack love seat. The grouping of four:
mother, brother, sister, me, arranged before the door,
a shadowy screen. My brother's stance, almost out of the frame,
legs spread, empty hands at his sides, his face red,
turned the other way behind black glasses.
The muddy canal beside us, someone's idea of scenery.

This would be the last time we vacationed this way, family of five.
We stand in a row squinting at the sun. Except for him,
my brother in his black Ray Bans. I'd forgotten how old
he seemed to me then. Eighteen, a grown-up, a man,
his acne cleared, his poker-straight hair slicked back,
the way it fell a little off center. Like him, aloof,
embarrassed, behind his two little sisters grinning.
Then his hands, their unclenched fists,
a grip on nothing. Like the wheel of the car that flipped,
the road beneath him becoming sky. But that came later,
a whole year, almost, to the day he didn't die.

★

Muscle and blood, and rocks by the sea. If I could live
my whole life outside, let the wind roughen my skin,
no—if I could become the wind, the brackish water's smell . . .

I should have been that son, first born,
even a name was chosen for me. My brother
came from somewhere else, from a man by now long dead
in Iowa. Nothing but flat fields and empty sky.
                                        My father
was a sailor with a faded blue anchor tattooed on his arm,
he had malaria, was a boxer. He grew up poor, quit school,
joined the Navy to see the world. The only book he ever read
was something by Steinbeck; he couldn't even say.
But he had read it a long slow time in the sick bay where
portholes rose and sank between two kinds of gray.

Now years later that father dead, the brother gone away,
I want the sea. There is in my suburban yard a little skiff,
weeds rooted in its faded tarp. I sailed it once so far alone
in an east-coast bay, I knew the size of life, about thirteen feet,
too small to go all the way. I want the sea, I want
the hard north wind inside me. This is romance:

to gaze out a window at a sliver of rooftop sky
and dream of the sea, of ferries crossing the bay
to where rocks go down, to where water turns night into day.

→>-<-

III

Elegy

Raw knuckles, pocket crescent:
envelope sky, blank paper moon.
The night is white; the moon, white,
milky as gristle against bone.

If I had a collar, I'd turn it up
against my neck, against the chill
mist falling. I shove my hands
into the rough denim mouths
full of hips. Shrink my neck,
perfect my hunch,
like yours, dead man.

I dreamed you under my hands
descending a stair, your back to my chest
slipping over and under the fluid tread
of the not-real. How heavy you were;
I knew then you were dead. Simple,
dream-logic; I distrust its *Let go.*

In November I held you, alive, just shy
of fifty, gray man. You slipped from my grip,
the cold an aura around you. Black raincoat,
shabby, familiar. Low slung pants. Paradoxical fashion:
the belly above, slim hips below. Familiar in passing.
Once, we danced a slow drunken slide; it was late
enough to forget whatever rules were to guide us.

Then you were hard against my thigh, the tender place
between bone and bone. The song ended:
we slid apart into different places in the dark.

If I could inhabit you, I would know how your wrist bones
slipped past cuffs. Why you never wore gloves.

The place where youth joints the aging paunch;
the story of the tumor in your groin, the scar tissue
that kept you out of Vietnam. Trees speeding past
as you left the exam. How alive you felt. How vivid they were.
If I could inhabit you, woeful man, squandering man,
I would know the press of raw knuckled flesh
into pockets familiar, warm. I could feel you gone.

→>-<-

The Boy in the Buckskin Suit

A boy in a buckskin suit went out
to hunt in a pastel woods
the size of the unknown world.
A boy gone off with a gun
had better know his way between
his home and his prey.

He tracked through trees as big as sky
a deer who ran and ran
and the boy kept up or fell behind
as the author wanted it.
The hunt both is and is not the story.

Out of the thicket he chased the deer
into a pool as deep and clear as an eye.
The deer disappeared.
The pool was wide, the current strong,
the spoiled gun encumbered him,
but still he swam, the gun upheld,
climbed out the other side.

In a dappled glade he slept
a timeless sleep.
When he woke, the sun was low;
his clothes, he felt, had dried.
He knelt above the dusk-tinged pool
to drink away his thirst.
Instead he gazed upon himself
in the only mirror he'd ever known.
The ringing trees shot back
his voice which cried: I have grown!

The way around the pool he found
was not so long at all,

and soon enough in a pencil-drawn field
rose up the cabin.
The gun faint with rust,
the shrunken skin that clutched
his boy's arms, boy's thighs,
pathetic sight. He stole humbly
to the porch beneath lamp's light
where his sister swept the floor.
He stuttered to her startled gaze,
"I've come at last from all these years,"
gangling arms uplifted.
In the yellow wedge of the open door
she said, "Foolish boy,
you've spoiled your suit
and father's gun.
Will you never be a man?"

→-◄-

Tohickon Creek in March

Too early now to stand naked on humped
shoulders of rock. The sky rings the color
of torrent: white water, whiter sky, empty
of sun. Come Easter, the first full moon
after the start of spring, Good Friday,
good time to hike to where grass snags
water's death, turned now to paper mats,
something woven by wind and rain.

Strip down, lay your clothes here on spears
of grass—pants, t-shirt, sweater,
seem to float above the bank
solid as canopy. Step down the mossy side
of boulder into water, swirling, colder
than sense can register. Wade in the pebble bottom
like the surgeon's tap before incision—something numb,
distant. Your skin grows tight or you expand within it.
The puckering, dimpling, like scales, or snakeskin
until you drop full weight into the flashing pools,
your heart for a moment a fist and nothing to punch,
and then your blood fast up to your head knocked back,
open eyes, mouth, lungs, this life.

⤙⤚

Seasons

➤ The Argument: Fire and Ice

First the fat man's voice, *Old lady,*
just get outside. The sound of glass, then thunder,
then the fist of flames. By noon the windows
are boarded, the street sullen as a black-eyed kid,
a smile slips around on the sandy ice,
then laughter plain and out of place.

Heat whistles through loose grates.
Last night, the engine's calming pitch,
idling, the long hoses recumbent.
In TV fires someone always stares
upward where someone else is sleeping
or calls from the window; no way inside.

The drama opens like a startled eye;
who must be restrained, who stands resigned?

➤ Bow River

The center has started to melt out toward the firs,
solemn as tapers at a wake. Chunks of blue,
splintery ice thrust up from the muddy bank
like raw glass, sapphire before the tumble into jewel.

From this bench at the bend, the river seems small,
all shadow now, the far March sun
in the clouds that shroud Tunnel Mountain.
Tracks crust over the surface ice.
I'd like to strip down to the skin, to plunge
into the river of snow, a knife in the heart,

a blade of flame to make the river run.
I listen for the creak that says thaw,
instead there's mockingbird and crow,
a short bright song of knowing when to go.

➤➤ Geography

No woods nearby, just a subdivision's scars,
down to the landfill's border
where bulldozers scrape poison
from the bottom of a lake. There's a sign
and a fence, and an open gate. Engines
grind tires through mud, and a smell
of something sweet and old,
more than thaw, comes from the pools
of thick grass. In twisted branches
a wasp's nest unravels like a mummy's head.
Even the clouds beckon, their black bodies
a charcoal map firm in the firmament,
a sea of dust, then the ground,
what's moving, what's standing still.

➤➤ This Is How to Love the Rain

One naked whip of forsythia
tamped into someone's idea of garden.
The air smells like dampened matches,
something between futility and beauty:
the flame against the tidy stick
like love (lighten me, devour me),
the breath of a kiss after sleep.

But how subtle the shades of gray
whitening into periwinkle, then dove,
or plover, to tuck our heads in its pearled wings.

All the world is water turned to something else:
the eye in its tears, the tadpole in its sac,
something glimmering, something going black.

→►◄←

The Name of the Place

This is really too long a story to tell,
I think, driving the old man along the Mersey River,
but I think it anyway sitting beside him,
his metronome leg keeping time.

Almost thirty years ago, I first came to this place.
There are constant reminders of who I was then:
who I am now, this eye without a face, without a head,
big as whatever it sees, becoming whatever it sees.
There is always a score by which action takes place,
and lighting. Then it was moody fog curled around trees,
fingering my summer clothes, seducing me with its faint,
fishy, smell, its salty coolness.
Now when I cross the river to see this old man
who folds his large frame into my small car
to drive with me to all the places he loves,
to give them to me, I remember.

Ferry Cross the Mersey, a title I never saw,
I heard as *Mercy*. It didn't need to make sense.
I thought, if I could have thought the word,
that it was metaphor: a boat across Mercy,
like Lethe or Styx. I was in sixth grade,
I knew something about myths. I sang and sang that song
that summer without a clue about the Mersey in England
matching a river in Liverpool, Nova Scotia.

Even now, this old man in my car, what to tell him?
Father of someone I loved, someone all caught up
with memory and landscape, what I mistook as fate:
A chance meeting, the name of a place. Never mind.
It doesn't matter, except that I came here
and met this father who saw the sea in my eyes—
tears for the love I'd missed, all jumbled up with the place.

He says I am one of them and I am, but not in the way
he means it. I cross the Mersey and cross it again;
no ferry now, just the car and the road we're on, humming.

→►◄←

Rock Gathering

Out of the sky—an upturned bowl—
recent steam, something empty, vaguely hissing.
It disappears like breath,
once drawn, forgotten;
one follows another, dumb, silent,
wordless as wind, water, day.

Break the tide-dried ribs of middle beach,
from ragged dunes to sucking shore,
crenellated chest, swollen belly,
a body traveled pointlessly;
walkway to sea, its own dead end.
Come, stop, look.
Turn to walk what seems endless:
fifty miles? sixty? ten?—
farther than the foot will go—
the eye bends like light
and disappears: land, mist, sky.

Walk enveloped in visibility,
smoky water white above itself:
seen, heard, the cold sand wet underfoot,
dangerous tug of open earth:
sole's imprint filled and gone.

Deep walking: spongy shoreline, silken sand,
the fine grains go to glass,
glass comes back turned and turned in water
back to sand. Lovers walk, heads down,
to find the pieces—
green, blue, brown, clear.
Prizes, souvenirs: they were here.

And then the rocks: sand came to rock,
and rock to sand. Handle them:
rose disk, palm-sized. Striated gray.
White cracked crystal lozenge.
Mica green. Rust-speckled egg.
Feel your pocket fill, lower, swing
against your belly, heavy against each step.
Sand underfoot; shimmering skin under skin,
glass into glass, rock into hand.

→>◄‹

At the Baptist Church

The way the light fell golden,
high in the maple trees
ringing Chimney Rock
between Black Mountain and Montreat,
as if driving steadily west
we'd get there, where the sun
still glowed, it could be, warmly
above the late afternoon's cold.

She said, *I want that light*
for a picture of you. And I drove
the open car, heater blowing,
up the steep gravel road
to the Baptist Church.
Its clapboard, the blue white
of skim milk against an empty cobalt bowl,
cast a shadow—sidewise glance—
into the trees' gray trunks.

I swung the car into that last light
before the wide white porch, the bolted door
and we kissed with our runny noses
and pinched cheeks there before the sleeping god
of blue-needle pines, of light too far to find.
And when we drew back to look beyond
the dark familiar altar of tongue
to peaked mouth nave, it was gone,
that longed-for light. And the high bluesy trees
whistled something that sounded,
I think now, like summer come again.

➤-◄

So We Go

Let's let the bay be the bay tonight,
whatever it is, say, mirror
seen between trees—
artily pink; glass, tinted.

There's this snow clumped—
fake as frosting on nylon boughs—
humped underfoot, frozen
on grass. What's left of undergrowth,

slick, the step less sure
for it. The light at dusk
a lure, a musk in our noses
so we go into it—the woods

still as the doe unseen
nearby; the dogs
quiver with her, but lack
the skill to track her.

We hush along the hidden path,
foot-blind, the water a halo
below this way, whatever it is
there and sure as tomorrow.

→>–<←

Persephone, Leaving

Now that I have soaked again
the feather pillows,
nightly shoulders for my tears,
I tidy the bed, fold the last remains of cloth:

what passed for clothing here—
where the encroaching cold
hastens me away.
Mother,
lover, two hearts break over me.

The alder turns its leaves to face the sky.
I leave, I cry, for a time, I die.

→>-<-

Acknowledgments

Grateful acknowledgment is made to the editors of the following publications in which these works or earlier versions of them have previously appeared.

The Antigonish Review: "Elegy with a Fiction in It," "The Name of the Place";
The Cortland Review: "Casual Man," "Homeward";
Emily Dickinson Award Anthology: "So We Go";
Excursus Literary Arts Journal Poetry Prize: "Dreaming of Anne Frank," "Like An Animal," "No Flowers," "Waking Late";
Many Mountains Moving: "Blame It on My Youth," "Seamless";
The Marlboro Review: "Elegy";
The Ontario Review: "Waiting for Fever to Pass";
Red Hen Press: "Seasons";
Tampa Review: "Tohickon Creek in March," "1967: White Point Beach";
Urban Nature: Poems about Wildlife in the City: "Outlook."

Special thanks to Stephen Dunn for selecting this manuscript, and to BOA for making it a reality after many long years of work. To Thom Ward for his gentle guidance and unerring sensibility and to Sarah Daniels for her patience and support. To the community of writers of the Warren Wilson MFA Program, my family and friends. And to Larry Levis, who truly heard my voice and encouraged me not to be afraid to speak my truths.

+>-<+

About the Author

Crystal Bacon is a 1995 graduate of the Warren Wilson MFA Program for Writers and a 1998 recipient of a New Jersey State Council of the Arts grant. As a Geraldine R. Dodge Foundation poet, she has led Clearing the Spring, Tending the Fountain seminars for teachers in southern New Jersey. Her work has appeared in a variety of publications in the United States and Canada, including *The Ontario Review, Tampa Review, Cortland Review, Marlboro Review,* and *Antigonish Review* as well as the anthology *Urban Nature: Poems about Wildlife in the City.* She has presented essays on Elizabeth Bishop in Massachusetts, Nova Scotia, and Ouro Preto, Brazil. These essays appear in *Divisions of the Heart: Elizabeth Bishop and the Art of Memory and Place,* and *In Worcester Massachusetts: Essays on Elizabeth Bishop from the 1997 Elizabeth Bishop Conference at WPI.* A Professor of Communications at Gloucester County College, she lives in Wenonah, New Jersey.

→►◄←

BOA Editions, Ltd.

THE A. POULIN, JR. NEW POETS OF AMERICA SERIES

Colophon

Elegy with a Glass of Whiskey, by Crystal Bacon,
with a Foreword by Stephen Dunn,
was set in Monotype Dante with Rococo Ornaments
by Richard Foerster, York Beach, Maine.
The cover design is by Dan Wangelin.
The cover art, "Whiskey," is by Chris Pelletiere.
Manufacturing by United Graphics, Inc., Mattoon, Illinois.

➤➤◄◄